Toddlers Tantrums

Understanding and Dealing with Toddlers Tantrums Effectively

By

Laura Harding

Table of Contents

APPROACHING TANTRUMS AND TODDLERS.................. 1

WHY IS MY CHILD HAVING TEMPER TANTRUMS?........... 3

TECHNIQUES FOR PREVENTING A MELTDOWN 6

PICK YOUR BATTLES, PREPARE FOR THE WORST 10

TANTRUM IN PROGRESS: WHAT TO DO AND WHAT
NOT TO DO.. 13

HOW TO DISCIPLINE EFFECTIVELY 17

LEARNING ABOUT CONSEQUENCES 18

SPANKING NOT EFFECTIVE AS A PARENTAL TOOL..... 23

PUTTING IT ALL TOGETHER 25

FINAL IMPORTANT NOTE: DON'T FORGET THE
POSITIVE!.. 26

Approaching Tantrums and Toddlers

You're at the end of your rope. It seems like the crying never stops. The tantrums begin with a powerful, "NO!" and end with tears and embarrassing, frustrating exits from social events and public places. You know that giving in and just giving your toddler want might pacify them, but you also know it's the exact wrong thing to do. What's a parent to do?

When it comes to toddlers and their behavior, it seems like every parent is an expert on the subject. All you need do to receive a barrage of unsolicited advice is to mention your child's latest outburst while in the company of similarly challenged, understanding parents. Ideally, along with the wealth of suggestions you may receive, you'll at least be the recipient of some knowing sympathy. It's a far nicer contrast to the unpleasant looks and comments you may be subject to in public with your child while they're acting out.

Unfortunately, that kindly, well-intentioned parental advice may not be very useful.

Parenting is an incredibly stressful, challenging job. It's understandable to look for outside help when it feels like your child is melting down on a regular basis. There are a few things that need to be emphasized before proceeding.

1. Temper tantrums are a normal part of child development.
2. Your child's temper tantrums do not mean you are a bad parent.
3. There are successful ways of addressing acting out.
4. What works for one child may not work for another.

While I believe all four points are of extreme importance, I can't emphasize the fourth point enough. As you read through this guide, understand that the suggestions you find in here may not suit your particular child and their needs. It is hoped that you will find suggestions that, when tried, work to help calm those periodic bouts of upset.

The approach we'll be taking in this book will be to focus on veer away from the scattershot methodology of crowd sourcing parental wisdom and focus on the science of child development. The sources for the suggestions found here will be trusted, authoritative sources. Within this book, we'll explore the reasons why your toddler is acting out, ways of mitigating that behavior, how to properly incorporate discipline.

Let's begin by getting to the heart of the issue by discussing why your toddler is acting out.

Why is My Child Having Temper Tantrums?

The play session seems to be going well. Your child is being friendly with other children, though still playing off by themselves. Perhaps they're even sharing. You've made it clear that you need to leave and tried setting expectations, but when it comes time to leave your toddler is starting to say no and cry.

Why is this happening?

As previously mentioned, temper tantrums are a normal part of growing up. According to the U.S. National Library of Medicine, temper tantrums begin at the around the ages of 12 to 18 months. These increase in intensity around ages 2 and 3 - parents know these ages as the "terrible twos" and, increasingly, the "terrible threes" - and are reduced after age 4. Bear in mind that they may not go away entirely at this age!

Though tantrums are normal and manageable, it's important to be cautious about them as well. There are cases in which you need to have your child work directly with a professional. The American Academy of Paediatrics suggests you should refer to a paediatrician or family physician in the event tantrums get worse after 4, if they hold their breath frequently, hurt themselves or others, destroy property, suffer from stomach aches, nightmares, and headaches, and regresses into earlier childhood behaviours. In fact, if you have any concerns at all regarding the intensity or the symptoms of tantrums, it's a good policy to consult a paediatrician.

Children with special needs and developmental delays may require further adjustment to the means and approach to discipline. Work with a paediatrician in this scenario as well.

For less extreme tantrum situations, emotional outbursts are a natural result of communication limitations. Your child's ability to communicate at this age is very limited and they've become frustrated. When they can't make themselves understood or when they can't emotionally accept the boundaries you have set, they respond in a way that they know will have your attention. It's an easy way to make their triggered anger known, and, perhaps, get the results they want.

There are other factors that come into play. Just like you, toddler's moods are impacted by their physical and emotional thresholds. Being overly tired, hungry, or thirsty can all more result in more severe tantrums, as can having already reached a certain level of frustration from a previous denial of the child's wants.

Speaking of hunger, if a child is older, able to communicate, and is possibly bored, you should find out if they are genuinely hungry or just bored. Like adults, sometimes children want to eat because they're bored. If they're hungry, definitely feed them. If not, a little redirection with an engaging activity might be all they need.

What a toddler wants may be unreasonable or simply directly oppositional to the boundaries being set. These emotional upsets can be triggered by extremely unreasonable demands, like wanting to run into the street or hit others. In those instances, it is natural that a parent or caregiver will need to physically intervene by holding onto the toddler and not giving them the ability to put themselves or others in danger.

Some of the things adults can do to deal with these naturally-occurring tantrums are to prevent the meltdown from ever occurring and by trying to work through the communication limitations. We'll also discuss how to deal with a tantrum as it's occurring.

One thing to definitely keep in mind at all times: you are the adult. Naturally, these situations can be extremely stressful and result in upset for the parent as well. You love your child and want the best for them. If you maintain a calm, adult attitude when your child is throwing a temper tantrum, you are going to keep far better control than you would if you show them you're angry as well.

Techniques for Preventing a Meltdown

How to Bridge the Communication Gap

If a great deal of your child's upset is a result of an inability to communicate, it stands to reason that bridging the communications gap should be a priority, if possible. It's true that communication won't guarantee that tantrums will end entirely. However, it might help to defuse some problems and reduce your child's frustration.

The following are some tips to developing those communication skills.

Language Development: From two years old and up, your child probably understands far more than they can say! They may have around fifty or more words. However, they may have difficulty using those words and it's far from certain that they can be understood outside of the family. This can be difficult and frustrating for your child.

Normally and over time, your toddler is going to develop their language skills just be listening and practicing. It may not seem like it, but little ones are constantly soaking up everything they hear and observe. At two, they're learning the basics of a story and are picking up some of what they're being read in books. Don't be surprised and alarmed if there's some delay. Children learn at a different pace. Girls may start earlier than boys, but it's not a definitive rule, so don't count on it.

If your child is having language comprehension or speech difficulties, be sure to have them examined for a physical exam and a hearing test. Early intervention is an important means of overcoming speech delays. Check with your local community to see if there are speech resources available for your child, if it's needed.

Baby Sign Language: One method for meeting your toddler's communication needs is to take up the practice of "baby sign language." This is particularly useful for children who aren't two or who are struggling with speech delay. The American Academy of Paediatricians approves of this approach as a means of "breaking the language barrier" and notes that it "really does deliver on its promise of improved communication."

While a baby from ages 6 or 7 months of age can begin to learn sign, they may not be able to use them until 8 or 9 months at about the age babies begin to understand what they want. They may also begin to really use the signs between ages 18 to 24 months- right at the time parents will most want to be able to communicate with their children.

While a child can learn the letters of the alphabet, at this age you will want to focus most strongly on basic concepts. A list of phrases suggested by the APP include airplane, baby, ball, bird, blanket, book, cat, cup, cold, daddy, diaper, dog, done, drink, eat, go, good night, happy, help, hot, hurt, I love you, milk, mommy, more, nap, no, outside, please, sit, sleep, star, thank you, up, water.

Expect that teaching and learning these phrases will take time! There should be no rush. Teaching and learning signs can be a creative, fun way of interacting with your child. The results will be much appreciated when your toddler is able to make it known to you that they're hungry, thirsty, tired, or need to be changed.

While learning and teaching these simple signs, it's essential to continue to work on helping your child develop speech. Baby sign is meant to assist, not replace vocal practice for hearing children. When your toddler has learned some of these words, it's important to share the signs with other regular caregivers. If your little one expects their sign to work with you, they'll certainly have the same expectation from others and could be very upset if they're unable to make themselves understood!

Discussing Moods: Your child's moods may change rapidly. That's natural. But one thing that can help is to identify negative moods, show empathy, and discuss what sadness is with your toddler.

For example, if your toddler is sad that they didn't get invited to a party, you might say to them, "I bet you were sad not to be invited to the party." Let them know that you know how they feel and give word to that emotion. Talk through the issue with your child and see if there is something you can do to make them feel less sad.
If your child is anger, don't tell them not to be angry. Suppressing emotions isn't natural or helpful. Instead, identify the anger and manage it, in particular if the child is behaving badly. You may say, for instance, "I understand you are angry about not being able to go to the playground. You can feel angry, that's okay. You can't scream."

There are ways of helping to let go of anger; exercises, calming music, and disengaging from the situation that caused the anger can be big helps in returning to a neutral mood.

It may well be that your own moods and behaviour are impacting your child. It stands to reason; we all affect one another with our moods and attitudes, and it can't be helped to some extent. If you are suffering from depression, consider consulting a professional if it is a persistent, recurring problem for you.

Pick Your Battles, Prepare For the Worst

You absolutely shouldn't give in to your child in every situation, nor should you be in a hurry to appease their every whim just to stop crying; this is universally true when the child is fully acting out, screaming, and acting out. However, there are some times prior to the tantrum when you may need to decide whether a screaming fit is worthwhile for a particular situation when a small appeasement will suffice. Decide whether you are being overly firm in that situation or whether you are correct to put your foot down in this instance.

It may be a tantrum that can be avoided based on your giving their request just a little more thought. A big blow up could be avoided if you simply think through the child's request and decide whether it can be accommodated or not. If so and it's not unreasonable, give them the benefit of the doubt.

Another approach is to offer choices. Sometimes, rather than giving an absolute "no," you could simply offer your toddler a choice between options that you approve of. This would give them a sense of having more independence and control over their own lives. This is often the major source of their upset rather than anything else.

If your child doesn't like the shirt you picked out for them, ask them if they'd like to help pick. Then choose from a group of shirts acceptable to you and let your child pick the one that they want to wear. Be sure you are absolutely okay with the possibilities. If this is a recurring fight, you could allow your child more say each morning by picking a few possibilities out and letting them help you decide.

There are times when you know your toddler is more prone to upset than not. Sometimes it just takes a small change. If you know that at times they get upset if they're hungry, bring snacks. If they are likely to be cranky from a lack of sleep, make sure they've had enough sleep the night before when possible. Try to be consistent about bedtimes whenever possible.

How much sleep does your child need? According to the National Health Service of the United Kingdom, At a year in age, your young toddler needs to have two hours and 30 minutes of sleep during the day and 11 hours of sleep a night. At two-years old, the nap time should be an hour and a half, while night time sleep should be 11 hours to 30 minutes. At age three, naps might be 45 minutes or not at all with 11 1/2 to 12 hours of sleep at night. By ages four and five naps are no longer suggested, while sleep time should be 11 1/2 and 11 hours respectively. Clearly, little ones need a lot of rest, and if they aren't getting it, this could be the cause of a particular outburst. Head those off with sleep when possible.

Knowing these signs of stress or overstimulation may be the difference between a major meltdown and simply walking it off. If you can take a child out of an over stimulating situation, even if it's just for a few minutes until they've had a chance to calm down, this may be all they need to recover.

A few other notes of prevention can work to help you out. If there are objects your child always wants to see and interact with and you can keep them out of their reach, do so. If you have more than one child and there are issues regarding dividing up things, make sure you're paying close attention to being "fair". Children have an early sense of what they deem to be fair, and will be quick to let you know if something isn't meeting their understanding of fair!

If you know that your child has a tendency to react badly to changes in routines, give them a five minute warning before the end of one activity. This is particularly important when the activity is something they have very much gotten into! If you are about to transition from home to going out, it's a great idea to pack a favourite toy or activity book for them, so they don't get bored. Boredom can be a cause of tantrums, so keeping the little one occupied while running errands can help a lot.

Tantrum in Progress: What to Do and What Not to Do

It's too late; you've prepared as best you can, tried all the techniques, but the tantrum is happening right now! We are in full meltdown status. I want to repeat that you may not have done anything wrong at all! Tantrums are a natural part of a child's development. Now we can focus on some of the do's and don'ts of handling your toddler's temper tantrum.

Do Stay Calm. This is the absolute key. Once a child is having trouble controlling their emotions, it's even more essential for you to be in control of your own. Be ready to handle this situation as best you can without losing your cool. We've already spoken about this earlier in the book, but it's a very difficult thing to do when your child is acting out, choosing not to act out yourself. Instead of becoming emotional yourself, remember that by staying calm, you are demonstrating to your child that they are not going to create a reaction from you. Don't stamp out of the room, replicate their behavior, or raise your voice. Your child will not understand what you're trying to accomplish and will feel that you are also not in control, which can be a very frightening emotion for a child. They expect you to be the calm when during their emotional meltdown!

If they're upset and you start getting upset, you may cause them to become even angrier. Don't feed into their anger by reinforcing it. Take a few deep breaths and you'll be able to show them acceptable behaviour with your own.

Tip: It's likely that you're going to get extremely frustrated by tantrums. However, it is essential not to lose your cool. If you ever feel you're about to snap or can't handle a situation, you absolutely should not give in. If at all possible, allow the other parent, partner, or family member to handle the situation.

Do Remind Your Child To Talk: Whether it's using sign or words, remind your child that whatever language skills they have can be put into play to say what they want. This is going to be most effective just before a tantrum, but could be attempted during the start of a meltdown.

There are no guarantees that this will work. Given that they may already be too emotional to hear you when you suggest using words, it's possible that this approach won't work in the moment. If so, don't press the point. It won't do any good and won't necessarily be heard.

Don't Give In! When the tantrum is in full force, this is not the time for negotiation or to give in. This lets your child know that their bad behavior will be rewarded. Giving in will open the door for future tantrum scenarios in which your toddler will absolutely anticipate that you will give in. Let them know that you're in charge and that you set the tone, not them.

Don't Allow Destructive Behavior: If your toddler is in danger of harming themselves or others or if they're damaging things, you need to immediately take them out of the situation and be prepared to help them calm down elsewhere. Be gentle when physically taking your child out of the situation, not aggressive.

Don't Walk Away: It may seem dramatic and strong to just walk away and let your little one act out until they've run out of steam. Do not do this. Apart from the fact that they would then be unsupervised and have no one watching over them if they hurt themselves, you need to stay with your child through the tantrum. The exception would be as previously stated, if you are absolutely at risk of becoming extremely emotional as well. In that instance, it's best to let someone else take over.

Instead, stay with the toddler so that you can work through the issues rather than letting them feel as though they've been abandoned and potentially increasing the intensity of the temper tantrum. As hard as it is to simply be there with the child while they're acting out, you need to be able to show that you are an ally for your child when this is happening and that you will be there with them through it. Many children, after the tantrum, feel strongly about how they've behaved, expressing remorse and regret. Your self-control lets them know they are safe and loved with you.

If it helps to remember, someone probably had to do the same with you! While all parents - including our own - weren't necessarily perfect with us when we were children, we should try to behave the least as we wish our parents had acted when we were confused by our feelings.

Don't Disagree! Naturally, parents, partners, and caregivers may have disagreements about how to discipline and deal with a screaming toddler, both in public and in private. However... this is not that time! Do not disagree with one another's parenting style at this time if you can help it.

By all means, have disagreements. Save those disagreements and those discussions for when you adults are alone, preferably when the child is sleeping. Talk it out then. There only needs to be one adult dealing with a tantrum at a time. If more than one adult is involved, they simply need to be on the same page. You don't want to give your child mixed signals by making them think one adult is going to give them what they want, while the other parent is "being mean." This is not a good situation to foster.

Do Connect With Your Child: After the tantrum has passed, discuss what's happened with your toddler. They may need to be assured that you understand their emotions and how they feel and that you are aware of their frustrations. Encourage your child to use words rather than screaming to get across what they wanted in future and, if you can't give them what they wanted, you may at least be able to work out something that would be acceptable to you and would make them feel better.

Above all, if discipline is employed make sure they know they're loved! A hug given when their behavior has improved lets them know that you're eager to reward for good behavior. Let them settle down before trying to talk anything through of course.

If you have other adult caregivers who aren't following your guidance on how to handle tantrums, this will send mixed messages for your toddler. Be sure that everyone on your team is on board with the idea of handling tantrums with cool, without giving in during the tantrum, and talking it through afterwards.

There will, of course, be times when discipline is necessary. Let's discuss those now.

—

How to Discipline Effectively

With all discipline techniques, it's important to bear in mind that certain techniques won't work with all children. For instance, if a child put in time-out is consistently getting angrier and acting out even more aggressively or refusing to stay in a time-out, you may have to consider another approach. Make sure that the discipline is age appropriate as well.

Though it can seem like they're the same thing, discipline isn't necessarily the same thing as punishment and control. The National Center of Biotechnology Information notes that while there is controversy about the right way to discipline, discipline is first and foremost about teaching, setting effective limits, and helping a child learn about self-control.

When considering discipline, remember that discipline should be solely handled by adults, never by other children in the family. It should be consistent and understood to be fair by the children (of course, they may not see it as fair at the moment of implementation). Discipline should lead to improvements in behavior and in understanding of the child's behavior. It needs to be constructive, not destructive.

The key concept is to make sure the child knows that there are consequences for their bad behaviors. Now let's talk about consequences.

Learning about Consequences

When it comes to consequences, age is an essential element to understanding. Realize we're talking about children who are at minimum 12 months old. Before this age, your baby can't comprehend consequences or discipline, as they have no means to plan ahead, be reasoned with, or recall what you may ask for them to do.

From ages 1 to 3, consequences can be very difficult. It's important at this age to teach some basic consequences. You can do this by making the child aware that there are natural and logical consequences.

When it comes to natural consequences, you can let the child learn what happens when something happens, conditional that they won't hurt themselves. For instance, if a child breaks a toy, let them know they can no longer play with the toy. Don't rush to rescue them from the consequences of their behavior by immediately fixing the item (though you certainly should take it away if it could harm them)! Let them learn the concept of cause and effect through experimentation.

Logical consequences are a little different in that you will be obligated to create a consequence. As another example, if your toddler refuses to behave and expects to play with a toy, that toy can be taken away as a consequence. Be calm about this; there's no need to raise your voice about the consequence. Just make it known that this is a normal consequence of that behavior, and they will begin to learn that bad behavior results in the loss of a toy.

When you are communicating with your child that they need to behave and how, keep it short. There's no need for complicated directions, in particular when a very short "no" or "no hitting!" will make your wishes known. This is simple and easy to understand, and will prevent confusion.

Redirection and Distraction

Exploration is a big part of this age, and as children try to discover their boundaries, they're naturally going to be upset when you enforce some required boundaries on them. This can be a big cause of meltdowns. However, you may be able to redirect that desire for exploration to a better purpose than breaking all of one's dishes.

Sometimes, no serious punishment is called for. With every young toddler, those who are between a year and two years of age, a means of disciplining may be to simply provide a firm, clear no. Take the child away from the object or area of interest and immediately redirect them with an alternative activity. One thing you have working in your favor in this area is attention span. Small children have limited attention spans, so it may be that the redirection will help take their minds off of what they want.

You'll want to keep a close eye on your toddler after the redirection to make sure they don't rush to the previous activity. Walking away and assuming everything will go fine is a recipe for problems.

For a child who's older than two, you may need to take the child away from the place where the tantrum began. As an example, if a child is in a public place, doesn't want to share their toys,, and is starting to throw a tantrum, pick them up and take them away from where they're acting out. Don't be aggressive or harmful; remain gentle. When they've calmed, a brief explanation of how they can behave correctly in future and provide an example of better behavior if possible.

Losing Privileges

When it's time to take something away, a privilege that needs to be taken away, try to connect it to the action. For instance, if your child is reacting over a specific toy, enjoyment of that toy could be the privilege that's revoked.

Privileges are exactly that; things that are non-essential to your toddler, but that they like and enjoy. You should never deny a youngster a meal as a consequence of their behavior, though you could take away a desert, of course.

Loss of privileges has less impact if they aren't taken away as an immediate result of bad behavior. If there is too much time between the behavior and the punishment, the child may not associate their actions with the punishment.

Be realistic about the punishments. Suggesting a child will lose a privilege "forever" is a meaningless threat. Taking away computer time for a day as opposed to "forever" is completely realistic, can be easily carried out, and has real meaning for the child. It's a good, strong consequence if that is something the child looks forward to in their day.

In the same way you didn't cave during the tantrum, don't give in and decide not to give the consequences. Carrying through demonstrates that tantrums are serious and are very undesirable for the child in future. Hold firm!

Time-Outs

Time-outs are a well-known and popular means of disciplining a child. However, they are most effective when used in response to a specific rule being broken. They are most effective between the ages of 2 and 5, though they can be used as a parental tool at any time.

While time-outs away from parents can be a good break on the parent's frayed nerves, it should be noted that young toddlers struggle with issues of abandonment. Their fears may make it best not to keep time-outs away from parents on a regular basis.

Make sure the time-out location is a known, expected spot. There should be no distractions in the location and they should not have a toy. This is a time and a place for calming down and getting de-stimulated, not to be rewarded with play.

Let your child know that there are certain actions and activities that will definitely result in a time-out; you may need to let them know several times so that it's fully understood. When the time-out has been warned about in advance follow-through. Make sure the teaching moment doesn't pass! The time-out length should be roughly one minute per year in age of the child.

When you start the time-out, make sure it happens immediately. When your child is in their time-out location, explain to them why they are there and do not allow them to wander off. If you must hold them in place gently to start, do so. Let them know that they're being held there for the time-out and don't hold further discussion, as you don't want to give your toddler the impression that they can negotiate their way out of consequences for their actions. If this is their first time-out, don't worry; future time-outs will likely be easier after they understand how time-outs work.

Time-outs shouldn't be used as a fallback for every time your toddler acts up. They stop being effective if you are simply forcing your child into the corner for a period of time. Instead, use them for those few, limited behaviors and only when other options aren't available such as redirection or talking through the problem.

When the time-out is over, they can go back to what they were doing. There's no further need for explanation or lectures. A hug will let them know they are loved, and is always recommended.

Spanking Not Effective as a

Parental Tool

Spanking and physical punishment aren't encouraged as a means to teach your child good behavior. The Women and Children's Health Network of South Australia provides a good example of the thinking regarding physical punishment; they note that physical punishment isn't the same as discipline, which is about teaching, not punishment.

Physical punishment undermines some key components of teaching children about good behavior. When a child feels safe and secure, they are much more likely to have a close relationship and to follow clear rules.

The American Academy of Paediatrics agrees. Spanking may have been a traditional means of deterring bad behavior; it has less impact over time. Physical punishment can increase both aggression and anger rather than teaching children how to behave.

It may be that the adult starts off intending to remain calm, but it's impossible to completely control one's emotions. One may start off calmly with spanking, but may then become less so; this could lead to a physical struggle with possible harm coming to the child. On the other end of the spectrum, a parent may not want to spank at all, so that when they do the physical punishment is less consistent and meaningful.

Corporal punishment can also be illegal in some places. As reported by the Global Initiative to End All Corporal Punishment of Children, 46 nations have prohibited corporal punishment from all settings, including the home. This prohibition includes all of Scandinavia, Germany, Spain, New Zealand, Portugal, the Netherlands, Hungary, Turkmenistan, and a number of countries in South and Central America, Africa, and Europe. There is an ongoing legal debate about corporal punishment in a number of countries.

There are other harsh punishments as well that should never be used, including name-calling and shouting. Don't humiliate your child as a means of punishment. NLBI warns that this sort of behavior will "make it hard for the child to respect and trust the parent."

Putting it All Together

We've talked about the reasons why your toddler is melting down, how to prevent and deal with tantrums, and what to do to properly discipline and teach your child about good behavior.

With all this advice, recall what was written earliest on; you know your child best. If something isn't quite working, adapt and adjust as is necessary for your particular toddler. Do understand that certain rules should be held firmly in place despite that need for flexibility.

You may, at times, give in to some emotional tantrums of your own as is natural within human nature. Just understand that this isn't productive or helpful. It's been said several times, but seriously- keep your cool! Show your child love and understanding, patience, and make sure that you model the behavior you want your little one to display.

It may seem like the easier path is to just let the child have whatever their heart desires. Who really wants to allow their child to get incredibly upset over a cookie when you could just as easily just give them what they want? But teaching your child self-control so that they aren't inappropriate, hostile, or endangering themselves or others is a loving part of parenting.

Final Important Note: Don't Forget the Positive!

Much of what we've talked about- given the subject matter- has had to revolve around the upset emotions of your child, accompanied by discipline. It's not always an uplifting subject. But if there's bad behavior, it can help to also reinforce the much positive behavior. A toy or a treat aren't always necessary rewards, either. Remember that sometimes all your little one needs is a little attention and a word of praise goes a long way.

If your toddler has learned the things that they shouldn't do and are taking actions to avoid the discipline that can be expected from doing those things- praise them! Let them know you're proud of them sharing, listening, and applying the lessons you've discussed. Staying positive can be a big boost in a child's confidence that they know how to meet your expectations.

Finally, if you enjoyed this book, then I'd like to ask you for a favor, would you be kind enough to leave a review for this book on Amazon? It would be greatly appreciated!

48094474R00019

Made in the USA
San Bernardino, CA
16 April 2017